Endorsements

"I think these questio .... stions gives students and thei .... :h answers that should genei ....ons that are individually relevant."

Paula M. Rooney   President, Dean College

"Ms. Dennis has given students **everything** they need to know about college—before, during, and after—priceless information at practically no cost! This will become the new "bible" for college-bound school students."

Marie L. Brown   CEO/Founder Forever & Ever Books

"I would endorse this book as a very good planning guide to any student or family member who wanted to know the lay of the land before they started their college journey."

Dr. James S. McCoy   Vice President for Enrollment
                      Management, University of
                      New Haven

"By asking a series of cut-to-the chase questions, *The New College Guide* helps students take control of the processes that most people find confusing and a little frightening. The book guides the reader on how to get into the right school, how to **make the most of college,** how to be smart about paying for it, and what to do after graduation. Answering the book's questions takes work, but students will be rewarded with the confidence that they are making thoughtful, informed decisions each step of the way."

Therese Kattner   Editor, *Recruitment and Retention*
                   in Higher Education

"Knowing the **right** questions to ask during the college admission process is a big challenge for prospective students and their parents. But no longer. They now have an insider's guide to the important 100 questions to ask and consider. Marguerite Dennis, a highly experienced admission executive, has given you a guide to lead your search process. The questions cover all of the obvious and not so obvious aspects of getting admitted to the right college for student and family. The questions are relevant for both a U.S. and international audience."

Michael Waxman-Lenz   CEO, International Educational
Advantage, LLC

"This book provides excellent insight into the college enrollment process from the perspective of an enrollment professional with over 40 years of successful enrollment experience in higher education. It helps parents, students, guidance counselors and international agents by providing a **practical perspective** to important enrollment issues that are critical in this life-changing event."

John W. Hamel   Assistant Vice President of Enrollment
& Director of Undergraduate
Admission, Suffolk University

"What happens when you can't afford a private college tutor, or you don't have the best guidance counselor? The **parents' role** in preparing their children for college has never been more important. The message in this book is clear: the right school is out there, you can get accepted, the cost will be manageable, and it's the smartest investment you can make."

Paul Burani   New father

"This book is **a must read** for anyone contemplating college. We are excited to give the book to our granddaughter, Emma, who will begin her college hunt next year."

Carol and Bob Seidler   Grandparents

"The New College Guide is a **practical and readable book** that addresses questions on the minds of millions of anxious students and parents not only in the United States but overseas. The book gives readers a golden opportunity to benefit from Marguerite Dennis' insights and wisdom about U.S. higher education gained from decades of professional experience."

Mark A. Ashwill, Ph.D   Managing Director, Capstone Vietnam & Former Country Director, Institute of International Education in Vietnam (2005-2009)

"A **simple and clear** way to understand the complicated and emotional process of choosing a college."

Mark Brown   Father of two pre-college children

Other books by Marguerite J. Dennis

Barron's Complete College Financing Guide

Keys to Financing a College Education

*Mortgaged Futures: How to Graduate
from School without Going Broke*

*A Practical Guide to Enrollment and
Retention Management in Higher Education*

Ten Trends in Higher Education

The New College Guide:
How to Get In,
Get Out,
and
Get a Job

Marguerite J. Dennis

Published by

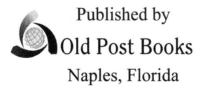 Old Post Books

Naples, Florida

The New College Guide:
How to Get In, Get Out, and Get a Job

by Marguerite J. Dennis

Copyright © 2014 by Marguerite J. Dennis

Published by

Old Post Books
PO Box 2725
Naples, FL 34106-2725
www.OldPostBooks.com

Printed in the USA

Library of Congress Control Number: 2014903027

ISBN: 978-0-9913918-4-4

Dedicated to

*Future college students and their parents,
high school guidance counselors and
international agents*

*With the hope that some of the questions
in this book will help you to select
the best college for you and for your family
and will help you to better guide
the students you counsel.*

Table of Contents

The New College Guide: How to Get In, Get Out, and Get a Job

INTRODUCTION

The focus of this book is not to teach you how to write the perfect essay or what extracurricular activities will catch the eye of an admission counselor. I am not going to tell you how many schools to put on your lists, how many campuses you should visit, or how to divide your lists among "stretch and safety" schools. I am writing this book as a college administrator but also as a parent who has been through the college application process twice. One of my daughters applied to five schools and was accepted to all of the schools. Another daughter visited twenty-three schools and while she was accepted to most, she was not accepted into her first choice school.

I am not writing for the 10 percent of students who, for a variety of reasons, will be admitted to the most elite schools in the country. I am writing for the other 90 percent of future college students who do not have the opportunity to hire private college tutors or whose guidance counselors have a caseload of 300+ students. I am writing from a lifetime of being on the other side of the desk and podium and knowing that the really important questions are not being asked.

I have taken what can be a complicated process and boiled it down to a manageable one. I will show you that there is a right school for you, that you can afford and that college costs can be managed. You will learn how to graduate in four years with manageable debt. And you will position yourself to find a job after you graduate. This is not impossible. We will do it together.

There are many books on applying to college, but this one is different. It guides you from the time *before* you apply to college, to the time *after* you are accepted, and finally to the time *after* you graduate.

This is hard work. Your journey cannot begin or end with the flip of a button on your computer. I am asking you to think seriously about yourself as a person, a college student, and a future worker. You cannot do that overnight. You should not begin this journey just before you need to send in your college applications. But it's never too late to begin. My mother was awarded a GED diploma at the age of 65 and when she reached her 90th birthday, she enrolled in her first college class! Please don't be discouraged or overwhelmed. Together we will go through the questions and eventually, you will be able to make a decision about the best college for you.

In the end, it is you who must, and should, make the final decision. Read the book carefully and get the answers to these questions. Be honest with yourself. The result will be enrolling in the best school for you, graduating in four years, and finding a job after graduation.

THIS IS WHAT I BELIEVE

There is a college or university for every student who wants to enroll.

There is a college or university that you can afford to attend.

You can graduate in four years, not five or six.

You can graduate with manageable debt.

You can position yourself in college to get a job after graduation.

International Students and Parents

Throughout this book, a globe symbol will designate important information for international students and parents.

The 100 questions in this book will help you select the college or university in the United States that is best for you.

Most international students cannot physically visit U.S. campuses before applying, so it is important to participate in virtual tours, whenever possible.

I recommend setting up a Skype account that will allow you to communicate with college and university officials in the United States.

Since international students do not qualify for United States' federal and state funding, you will need to investigate the specific funding options from your country or relatives.

You may wish to remain in the United States after graduation for Optional Practical Training (OPT). This allows international graduates to work to gain valuable work experience before returning home.

———•———

It's time to begin this journey together. The 100 questions in this book are divided into three parts, as listed below. The chart at the end of the book includes all the questions for easy reference, along with suggestions for finding the answers.

PART 1 - Before you apply to college –
Pre-Application Stage – Questions 1-42

PART 2 - After you are accepted to college –
Post-Acceptance Stage –
Questions 43-94

PART 3 - After you graduate from college –
Post-Graduation Stage –
Questions 95-100

PART 1

PRE- APPLICATION STAGE

I put a great deal of emphasis on getting as much information as possible *before* you spend the time and money applying to multiple schools. This section of the book is designed to help you narrow your focus to those schools that best meet your academic needs and that your family can afford. The questions in this chapter may be the most important ones in the book. Take the time to consider each question carefully.

Question 1: Where Do I Want
To Go to School?

School Location and Size

Decide if you want a rural, suburban, or city location and if you want to travel more or less than 500 miles from home. This will help you to narrow the number of schools on your list and to focus on the options. Many students and parents want the comfort of being able to visit each other regularly. Others may be excited by the possibility of going to school in another part of the country or world.

Do you want to enroll in a large or a small school? Both have advantages and disadvantages. It's important to ask yourself if you would feel more comfortable in a first- year class of 300+ students rather than in a tutorial-style class of 20. Remember this is not a test. There is no right or wrong answer. It is a matter of individual preference. By deciding the size preference of your prospective school, you will begin to narrow your choices and focus on a specific number of schools.

When my youngest daughter began her college search, we travelled to 23 different schools. She enrolled in the first school we visited. We could have saved a lot of time and frustration if we had asked this first question before we began our road trip.

Question 2: Do I Want to Go to a College or a University?

Type of School

This can be a tough question to answer. Few college students know exactly what their future career will be. At some of the best schools in the country, students are not even allowed to declare a major until the sophomore year. Maybe you are not sure of the difference between a college and a university. The dictionary defines a college as an institution of higher learning that grants bachelor's degrees. A university is defined as an institution of higher learning with teaching and research facilities composed of a graduate school, professional schools, and an undergraduate division.

Colleges tend to be smaller in size than universities, so how you answered the first question may help you to answer this one. If you know you want to be an accountant, by all means focus on universities with strong accounting programs. If you know you want to be a doctor, you could consider colleges and universities since both offer pre-med programs; however it would be important to investigate the medical school placement rates of each school on your list.

Question 3: Do I Know What I Want to Study?

College and University Majors

How you answered Question # 2 will influence how you answer this question. Keep in mind that the average college student will change majors at least once and that few college students have a clear idea of how they want to spend the rest of their working lives. For those reasons, I suggest you consider schools that offer a wide variety of majors. It's wise to enroll in broad-based liberal arts courses during the first year. Also plan on spending a lot of time with your first-year advisor who will help you explore the many available options to help you make good choices. In the first weeks and semesters of your academic career, an engaged academic advisor can be extremely helpful as you decide on a major and plan your courses.

Question 4: Am I a Good Student?

Honors Programs

I have known students who rejected colleges and universities because they did not have honors programs. Most of the best schools in the country, however, offer honors courses to academically talented students, including special seminars, research opportunities, and study abroad programs. Typically, honors students are awarded generous institutional grants. If you have out-standing grades, by all means consider schools with honors programs.

International students are also eligible for funding if accepted into an honors program.

———•———

Question 5: What Are Students Studying?

Most Popular Majors

The answer to this question is usually not found in college view books or on websites. Some college and university guides will list a school's most popular majors. But to find out why these majors are so popular you will need to dig a bit deeper. This may be a good time to e-mail or call the admission office of each of the schools on your list. If you have the answers to Questions # 1 and #2, the list should be manageable. Find out from the admission counselor why the majors listed are popular, and then continue your investigation by contacting the department chair and asking the same question. The answers should match.

You may be thinking, even at this early stage, that this is just too much work. Remember that one out of every three college students does not graduate from the first school they entered and 50 percent never graduate. By doing the work *now* you will save time and money *later.* You don't want to become a dropout or transfer statistic.

Question 6: Will I Meet Students from Other Parts of the United States and World?

Diversity

This is a personal preference and there is no right way or wrong way to answer this question. Are you more comfortable in a class where most of the students are the same as you or do you want to meet students from out-of-state or from another country? This is a personal preference, and there is no right or wrong way to answer the question.

A diversified classroom, full of students from different backgrounds, can add a great deal to your learning experience. It's OK if you prefer a more homogeneous group of students. It's OK if you want to enroll in a school with a specific religious affiliation. It's OK if you want a school with a strong Greek system of fraternities and sororities. It's OK if you want a school with a major sports program. It's also OK if you are interested in a school with a competitive debating team or service learning programs.

The print and online publications for most colleges and universities list the diversity of the student body. They also include information about any fraternities and sororities, sports programs, etc.

If you are an international student be sure to find out about the cross-cultural opportunities for each of the schools on your list as well as the number of international students enrolled and the number of students from your country. Some international students flock to U.S. schools with large international student populations and a large number of students from their own countries. Other international students are more interested in meeting American students. There is no right or wrong answer. This is an individual preference.

―――――•―――――

Question 7: How Big Is Big for First-Year Students?

Average Class Size

Most of the information on class size gives the average class size for *all four years.* That means that the 300+ freshman class is averaged along with the 25 students in a senior class in advanced statistics. What you want to know is the average class size for all *first-year courses* .That will give you a better idea of the attention you will get in the first year.

Question 8: Who Will Teach Me?

Full-time Faculty, Adjunct Faculty, and Graduate Assistants

I believe the classroom professor is the most important factor in student success. I also know that many schools do not have their "best," full-time faculty teaching freshman students. According to a recent report, 50 percent of all professors at four-year colleges are part-time adjuncts. Adjunct faculty and graduate teaching assistants cannot, in my opinion, provide the same kind of educational experience and academic advising that a full-time professor can provide.

There are many excellent adjunct professors and good graduate teaching assistants, but I do not believe that they are assigned to teach first-year students only because they are good teachers. Most schools use adjuncts and graduate students to save money. The best colleges and universities will put their best teachers in freshmen classrooms.

Question 9: May I Sit in on Classes Before I Apply?

Classroom Visit

If you have narrowed your choice of schools to visit before applying, why not take the time to sit in on a few classes when you visit? Most future college students and parents dutifully attend the "sales pitch" by the admission office staff and dutifully follow the walking backwards tour guide. All this is important, but I suggest that after the tour, you arrange to visit at least two classes. Try to sit in on a first-year class and a more-advanced one. This will add another layer of information that you cannot get from official presentations.

I would pass on the lunch offered by the school and visit the cafeteria. Maybe you could ask the students having lunch what they think of their school? Look for the match-ups between the images the school is projecting and the answers of the students you meet in the cafeteria.

If you are an international student, you will probably not have the option of traveling from one American school to another. Make the most of virtual tours and Skype interviews.

------•------

Question 10: How Many Freshmen Become Sophomores?

Progression and Graduation

Students who leave school for a semester or year either will never graduate or will take longer than four years, costing both time and money. But the first question to ask is the percentage of students who enter the second year. This is the more important question for you to ask at this stage of your college investigation. The answer will tell you how well students are advised and counseled during the first year.

Question 11: How Long Will It Take Me to Graduate?

Graduation in Four, Five and Six Years

Not only do you want to know the percentage of freshmen who become sophomores, but you also want to know, by major, the percentage of students who graduate in four, five, and six years. You want to ask what "guarantees," if any, the school offers to students who do not graduate in four years. Is the fifth year free? You want to know if your academic advisor can give you an "academic map" of the courses you need to follow that will put you on track to graduate in four years. Don't wait until after the first semester to get this information. Your "academic map" is critical if you want to graduate on time. Graduating on time means graduating in four years, not five or six.

Question 12: How Many Credits Do I
Need to Graduate?

Graduation Credits

Most first- year students don't decide what courses they will study in the first semester and first
year. They are assigned classes either by freshman
advisors or by a cookie-cutter registration system.
And most freshmen are assigned four courses (totaling 15 or 12 credits). If the four courses total
12 credits, then it is mathematically impossible to
graduate in four years since most schools require
120+ credits to graduate.

Many years ago, in my first administrative job
when I was a student at St. John's University in
New York, I had to assign classes to incoming
students. Each student took six courses, totaling
18 credits. Most of us were commuters, and the
classes had to be assigned close together so that
we could get to work after school. Over 95 percent of the students took 18 credits, commuted to
school, and worked 20 hours. No one would think
of taking more than 4 years to graduate. We sim-
ply could not afford an extra year or two of school
and most of us had parents who would not have
supported extra time in college. We had a limited
amount of time and money to spend in college before we had to work full-time.

Please decide today that you have only *four years* to spend in college. You will not regret this decision.

Ask for a "typical" freshman schedule and find out if it is possible to add or substitute classes. Most schools charge a flat fee for up to 15 credits. Find out how many credits are needed to graduate. Ask if there are language or study abroad requirements. Remember that you are the customer/student. Find out how the schools on your list will help you to graduate in four years.

Question 13: Do I Have Research Interests?

Research with Faculty

I may be getting ahead of you with this question, but for some students, it is important to know that research with faculty is possible. You may be one of those students. Maybe your guidance counselor has encouraged you to apply to a particular school in order to follow your research interests? There is nothing wrong with getting information on faculty research projects or grants. This can be true for many majors, but it can be especially important for science students. This information could be a deal breaker for you. It can eliminate some of the schools still on your list.

Question 14: How Can I Manage Classes in the First Year?

Academic Support Services

The first semester of college can be the most challenging and confusing. Whether you are a commuter student like the majority of college students, or a residential student, there are many new skills you need to learn to help you navigate through the first semester and year. Time-management skills are important. So is finding and assembling your own academic team. This means taking a pro-active approach to your first semester and not a passive one.

Professors in each of your classes should distribute a list of reading assignments, class projects, terms papers, mid-term and final exam schedule, etc. With this information you should determine how best to manage each class. For example, if a class has no mid-term exam and only one final test, you may want to schedule an appointment with the professor to get feedback as to how you are progressing. No final grade should come as a surprise. If you know you do not understand the material or do poorly on the mid-term exam, immediately seek the services not only of the professor, but also of the school's academic support staff or tutors.

Understand clearly what happens if you have a grade point average (GPA) below 2.0. That is the minimum GPA you have to achieve to graduate. Understand clearly how adding or dropping a course can impact your first-semester grades.

Once enrolled, get to know the staff in the registrar's office. Ultimately, someone in that office will sign off that you have completed all of the necessary requirements for graduation. Ask for a "senior" audit to be done for you at the end of your sophomore and junior years. Do not wait until your final year to find out that you cannot graduate because you don't have the required number of courses.

International students will want to have a list of the specific services for students for whom English is not their first language. There are many excellent programs for students who may not meet the English requirements for admission.

Maybe you think getting this kind of information is not important at this stage in your search. Trust me. This is important. Take the time and get this information. It is a ticket to your graduation.

Remember in Question #3, I emphasized the importance of the academic advisor in freshmen year? If the schools still on your list do not have specific academic support services, or first-year academic advisors, you may want to re-consider these schools. The first semester is when you need the most help and when the school should offer the most academic assistance. The first semester sets the path for all the semesters that follow.

Question 15: What Are My Interests?

Student Services

College is not all about work, getting good grades, getting a job after graduation, etc. That is only one part of the college experience. This is also the time to explore the person you are and want to become. It is a time to enjoy the extracurricular activities most colleges and universities offer. It is a time to take whatever talents you have to another level. At this stage of your college exploration, take a look at the student services offered by each of the schools on your list. Is there a match with your interests?

I always ended my presentation to future college students by inviting them to look back on their college years as the best time in their life! That is what I wished for them and what I want for each of you. What happens outside the classroom is a contributing factor.

International students should learn the specific student services available for them. Is there a special orientation for international students and parents? Is there a special international student-service program? This may not be important for some international students. For others this information could be a deal breaker.

Question 16: Who Is Talking with Me?

Communication with Students

Some of you reading this book may agree with me that most of the view books sent to you (unsolicited) end up in the re-cycle bin. Admission counselors often forget that the "digital natives" of today do not want generic, one-size-fits-all communication. Some of the best admission and enrollment programs have a communication plan that really informs families about the distinctive benefits, not just features, of their school. Get this information before you enroll.

Communication is not only from the admission staff. Presidents, deans, coaches, current students, and alumni should all be part of the information flow. After acceptance and enrollment, this kind of communication should continue from the dean of students' staff, the career counseling staff, and even the alumni staff.

Question 17: Who Is Talking with Parents?

Communication with Parents

Any parent reading this book should be receiving regular and frequent communication from all of the schools under consideration. How many schools have parent communication programs from the time of application to the time of enrollment? Not many, I'm afraid. What I am writing about here is communication that is parent-specific.

Not many future college students are interested in a school's bond rating but some parents may be interested. That is one criterion indicating a school's financial stability and viability. Not many future college students are interested in a four-year calendar. But for parents, who want to make travel plans and/or schedule family vacations, this is important information. This is especially true for families where there is a great distance between parents and school. Not many future college students ask for the nearest local hospital. But in my experience, many parents ask that question. You get the point. There are questions that are important to parents that are separate and distinct from those important to students.

Question 18: How Safe are the Schools on My List?

Crime Rate

You may not know that federal law (Cleary Act) requires all colleges and universities in the United States to make available to the public the crimes committed at and/or associated with their schools. Maybe that is not a big deal for you today, but if a school has a record of assaults or rapes, shouldn't that figure into your selection process? Future college students and parents should make sure to ask about school safety and check the college website for a list of crimes.

Take a look at each school's campus security program. Is there a shuttle bus? Does the school offer an escort service? Find out if there is limited access into dormitories. If you have a car, register it with the campus security department.

College is a time for growth, exploration, transition and yes, fun. You should not spend any time looking over your shoulder after a night class or in the parking lot. Get the information now so you won't be sorry later.

Question 19: Why Should I Attend Your School?

Specific Reasons

This is a good time to ask this question. Admission counselors, deans, and other school officials may answer by talking about small class sizes and individual attention. But hundreds of other schools also have small size classes and provide individual attention. What makes this school different from all the others and better for you? If school officials cannot give specific reasons why you should attend their school, it's time to investigate further or delete the school from your list. There has to be more specific reasons why you should enroll.

If you are an international student ask why you, as an international student, should attend this school.

———•———

Question 20: Why Are Students Leaving?

Transferring Out

If the statistic is true that one out of every three college students will not graduate from the school they enter, then you have a good chance of leaving the first school you enter. For each school on your list, find out the transfer rates, by major, after one semester and also after one year. Also find out why students transfer. Remember most transfer students do not have all of their credits transferred to their next school, and that translates into more time in school.

There is something called "reverse transfer" that is a trend today. Students start at a four-year school, leave for academic or, more likely, financial reasons, enroll in a two-year or community college, and then return and graduate from a four-year school. Find out why students leave. Getting this information before applying may save you disappointment later on.

Question 21: Why Are Students Enrolling?

Transferring In

Are students transferring into any of the schools on your list? The answer to this question is as important as the answer to Question #20. There may be a very positive reason why students enroll in one college after starting out in another school. Find out the reasons why students transfer into the schools still on your list. This may be a good reason to keep a school on your list.

Many colleges and universities in the United States have international articulation agreements with international schools. If you are an international student find out which schools have these agreements. You might want to spend two years studying in your own country and then transfer to an American school. Most of your credits will transfer because the two schools have a written agreement.

Question 22: Will I Fit In?

Typical Student

Who is the typical student at each of the schools you are considering? Is there a typical student? Should there be? There are several college guidebooks that can help with these questions.

But I would go further and ask an admission counselor for a definition of the typical student. Knowing that, can you picture yourself in this school? Do you think you would feel comfortable? If you have no interest in sports, but several of the schools on your list are sports-obsessed, would they be the best fit for you? If you are a big sports fan but have only Division III schools on your list, would they be the best fit for you? This is an individual choice. You cannot fail Question# 22. But you do have to answer it honestly. No one can do it for you, not a guidebook, guidance counselor, parent, etc. Spend some time on this question. It's an important one.

If you are an international student, ask who the typical international student is. Compare yourself with the answer you get to this question. Is there a match?

Question 23: Will I Graduate?

Profile of Students Who Graduate

This is a rarely asked question. Once you have a clear understanding of why students leave a school, find out why they stay. What are the personality characteristics of students who successfully navigate the waters at each school on your list? Do they match your personality? Is the school able to provide you with this information? My guess is that many schools cannot. But you have the right to ask this very important question.

What is the profile of the international student who is successful? Compare this information for all of the schools on your list.

Question 24: What about Advanced Degrees?

Graduate and Professional School Placement

I really am not getting too far ahead by putting this question here. According to a recent article, a bachelor's degree today is what a high school diploma was forty years ago. If you compare the starting salaries and unemployment rates for students who have undergraduate degrees only, with those for students who have both undergraduate and graduate degrees, the evidence is clear. Graduate and professional school students have higher salaries and lower unemployment rates.

If you don't know what you want to study in your first year of college, that's OK. But do find out the graduate school and professional school acceptance rates for each of the schools still on your list.

It's OK if you feel overwhelmed by some of these questions. Maybe you thought you had a clear idea of where you wanted to go to school? And maybe some of the questions changed your mind? Maybe you had a list of 25 schools when you began reading these questions and maybe that list is now down to 10? That's OK. I will have accomplished my purpose: to save you and your parents time and money *before* you apply to college.

Let's take a break. I think you have earned it. Come back refreshed for Question # 25. But I warn you. The next 11 questions focus on college financing and affordability. You may want to delete some of the schools on your list because of "sticker shock." Don't do it. Remember that the published tuition is not what the majority of families pay.

In this next section of the book we will cover: financial aid awards, net price calculators, student debt, parent debt, and loan forgiveness programs. *Do not eliminate a school only because of cost.* If you do your homework you may discover you can afford a school that once seemed unaffordable. Let me be very clear: *I honestly believe that there is at least one college or university in the United States that you can afford to attend!*

Parents should pay particular attention to the next 11 questions. You will probably have the greatest influence in determining whether, as a family, you can afford one school but not another.

Question 25: Can I Afford This School?

Tuition Increases

Now is the time to determine if your family can afford the schools still on your list. First, make a list of the tuition costs of each school you are considering. Then contact a counselor in the admission or financial aid office, and ask what the average tuition increases have been for the past five years and what they are projected to be in the next four years. Average annual tuition increases for private schools range from 3% to 5%.

It is more difficult to project tuition costs for public schools because state legislators set tuition rates. Knowing that in-state tuition and fees at public schools increased only 2.9 percent in 2013-14 should be a useful guide.

Question 26: Are There Other Costs Besides Tuition?

Other Costs

Remember, tuition is just one part of total college costs. If you plan on being a residential student, you want to know the increases in dormitory rates from year to year. You will also need to factor in book costs, health insurance, and living expenses. What is the total bill likely to be? Add that information to the tuition costs from Question # 25 and this will give you the total amount it will cost to attend each school on your list.

Be careful when calculating total costs. Most public schools have lower tuition costs than private colleges and universities. But due to recent cuts in state aid, tuition and fees at many state schools have increased more than in some private colleges. After you do all these calculations, the total costs may be similar.

Here are some suggestions for cutting costs:

- Attend a two-year college, and then transfer to a four-year school.
- If you are able, enroll in online courses before you begin college.
- Take as many AP or IB courses as possible.
- Commute from home to school.
- If you can, graduate in three years.
- Plan to work before you enter college and while you are enrolled in college.
- Consider schools that have cooperative-education programs.

Question 27: What Kind of Financial Aid Is Available?

Average Financial Aid Package

You will need to have a conversation with someone in the financial aid office to get this information. If you live near any of the schools on your list, make an appointment with an aid counselor and bring your parents with you. During your visit, ask for examples of sample financial aid packages. The financial aid counselor may even be willing to estimate the amount and type of aid – federal, state, institutional grant and loan – that your family could be awarded based on your family's income and your grades. Now the picture gets a bit clearer. This information will help you figure out whether you can afford to attend this school.

I know of one school whose staff meets with families in the evenings and on week-ends and computes the affordability for each family. Families know *before* they even apply if they can afford to attend this school. Talk about customer service. Find out if the schools on your list can estimate what your financial aid is likely to be *before* you apply.

If you cannot physically visit each of the campuses on your list, arrange a Skype interview or telephone call. Question # 27 is very important and may reduce the number of schools on your list.

International students should get information on all institutional aid available to non-U.S. citizens.

Question 28: Are There Tools to Help Me Calculate the Total Cost of Attendance?

Net Price Calculators

Federal law requires each school to give prospective students and parents a net price calculator, allowing the family to determine the cost of attendance. The jury is still out on the effectiveness of this tool. My advice: it can't hurt to do the calculation and the results may show how your family could afford this school but not that one.

Wouldn't you rather know *before* spending the time and money to apply that you have no chance of managing the costs? Wouldn't the admission officer want fewer, but more realistic applicants? There were many times, over the course of my administrative career, that I had to tell students that they could not afford to attend my school. That was the right thing to do even if the advice was not always followed.

Question 29: Will I Receive the Same Amount of Financial Aid Each Year I Am in School?

Bait and Switch

Not many families ask whether the financial aid awarded in the first year will continue after freshman year. Some schools give generous financial aid packages to freshman students that look a bit different in the second year, even if the family's income has not changed. For example, the ratio of loans to grants may have changed. The total amount might be the same, but the loan bill might have increased.

Please be certain to get this issue clarified not only by admission counselors, but also by financial aid staff. Many schools assign incoming students a financial aid counselor who will remain their counselor for all four years. Ask whether the same person will be awarding you financial aid each year that you are in school.

Question 30: Will I Have to Pay Full Tuition?

Sticker Shock

Not every student pays full tuition. Most private colleges and universities, and many public schools, offer generous grants. Some of the scholarships are based on grades, some on financial need. Check with all of the schools on your list to learn of their grant programs. Also reread Question # 29 about bait and switch to be certain that if you are awarded grant funding, it will apply for all four years.

Question 31: Does Everyone Get Financial Aid?

Percentages on Aid

Find out the percentages of students in first, second, third, and fourth years who receive financial aid. Again you want to be certain that the aid you receive for the first year will follow through until graduation. Your aid should not change if your family income has not changed. You should dig further and compare the percentage of your aid package that is grants and the percentage that is loans.

Do the schools on your list award merit scholarships and scholarships for different majors? Ask how much aid was distributed to each school by the federal and state governments. If there are several schools on your list that are state schools, ask about the reduction in state aid and how the school has made up the deficit. Did tuition or fees increase? I bet they did.

If you are an international student find out the percentage of international students who receive institutional aid for each of the schools on your list.

———•———

Question 32: Will I Have to Take Out Loans?

Student Debt

Don't believe the media hype about student debt. About two thirds of all college graduates have some; however less than 1 percent owe more than $100,000, 40 percent owe less than $10,000 and 30 percent owe between $10,000 and $25,000. The average student debt at graduation last year was $29,400.

You and your parents should decide how much you are able and willing to borrow for college and then check your list of schools. Remember there *is* a school that is affordable for every family. The work you are doing right now will help you discover school(s) that your family can afford. Sharpen your pencils, and keep the schools on your list that are within your family's financial reach.

International students also need to calculate the amount of debt they will have by the end of senior year. The loan sources will be different from those for American students, but the result can be just as devastating if too much money is borrowed for college.

Question 33: Will My Parents Have to Take Out Loans?

Parent Debt

We read about average student debt, but that amount does not take into account what parents borrow to put their children through school. With home lines of credit and retirement funds not as readily available as they once were to finance college, parents are unable or less willing to incur large college loan bills.

You and your parents should add up the following for each school on your list: average total costs, average aid package, average grant, and average loan. To those figures subtract the money in your college savings account (if you have one), and the estimated amount of money you can earn from employment in the summer and during the academic year. Look at the financial "gap." How much are parents willing to contribute to make the "gap" disappear?

Now is the time to determine this, not *after* enrollment. Spend the time to calculate family, not just student debt. Then share your family's calculations with an admission or financial aid counselor at the schools still on your list. Maybe there is some other way to make the numbers work?

Maybe you will have to commute for one or two years? Maybe you will join a school that offers a cooperative-education program? Maybe the school can increase your financial aid package?

What I am suggesting requires a lot of work and family cooperation well before applications are submitted. But it is worth it. Trust me. If you *really* want to attend a particular school, make it work. I know this is possible because I made it work for many families over the years.

Most international parents finance their child's college education through savings. However, if that is not possible for your family, your parents will have to determine if they want to borrow for college.

Question 34: How Do I Know If I Am Borrowing Too Much?

Loan Limits and Starting Salaries

Here's another good question to ask: do the schools on your list set loan limits and are the limits tied to starting salaries? Some of the best college financial counseling programs will do this. The concept is getting some traction at federal and state levels. Ask the question, especially if you are certain of your major. Starting salaries will differ in different parts of the country and world. Try to get information specific to your area in the United States or world.

Question 35: Is There Some Way to Reduce My Loan Bill?

Loan Forgiveness Programs

I knew a school that developed its own loan program. The interest rate was 3 percent. This is a very attractive loan, and the terms were even better. The day the students who borrowed under this loan program graduated, the loan was forgiven. This provided a great incentive for students to stay in school. One year, the graduation rate for this group of students was over 75 percent. Ask if this type of loan or similar options, are available at each of the schools on your list. You have nothing to lose by asking the question. Colleges and universities are getting better about offering attractive financing options to families. Remember you want to graduate in four years. Colleges and universities want to keep you enrolled for four years. A high, four-year graduation rate makes everyone happy!

There are federal and state programs that will forgive a portion of your loan if you work in a particular area or designated major. Medical and law school graduates, for example, will have a portion of their loans forgiven if they work in an underserved area. Your financial aid counselor can provide information on all loan forgiveness programs. Federal and state websites can also provide information on specific loan forgiveness programs.

Question 36: Is It Possible to See Samples of Financial Aid Award Letters?

Online Financial Aid Award Letters

Ask if sample financial aid award letters are posted online. This will help you and your parents determine whether your financial calculations and the sample awards match. Please *never* delete a school based *only* on finances. I know many families look at the sticker price and turn the page. But if you ask Questions 25 through 36, and you compare the answers, the financial picture may change. You may be surprised. It may be cheaper to attend the private school near home than the public university far away from home.

I may be wrong, but I bet at this point in your college search, you have at least five schools on your list. It's OK if you have more or fewer than that number. Remember this is your search, not mine.

I don't know about you but I am ready for a break. Spend some time thinking about the questions listed so far. Please remember that you are still in the PRE-APPLICATION STAGE. You have not turned in one application yet! Hopefully, you won't until you get the answers to at least some of these 36 questions. If you are having a hard time getting all the information yourself maybe you can divide the questions between you and your parents or you and your spouse, if you are an adult learner?

When you return we will focus on employment after graduation. You read that last sentence correctly. You are not yet in college and I am asking you to fast forward to college graduation. Come back from your break and you will learn why.

Question 37: Who Can Help Me Find a Job?

Career Counseling

All recent surveys of parents and students focus on college affordability and return on investment (ROI). ROI really means a job after graduation. Most families do not believe that schools are doing enough to help students get jobs after graduation and along with affordability, career counseling is the most important consideration in college selection.

I know from my own administrative experience that career counselors never had a seat at the table when enrollment plans were written; career counseling was not a part of any plan. Even today some college presidents believe that career counseling is not important and that young (and older) people should attend school for the joy of learning and to develop intellectually. I agree with that. But I have yet to find a happy, unemployed college graduate or happy parents who are paying large loan bills while their child surfs the web for employment.

Career counseling cannot, and should not, begin when you are a senior in college. Some of the best schools in the country offer seminars and guidance to students in the very first year. Obviously the information you get during freshman year is different from what is presented during senior year. But I believe, given the grim worldwide unemployment and underemployment statistics, you cannot get too much guidance.

Ask about employment statistics at the time of graduation for each of the schools on your list. What kinds of jobs are graduates getting? If nothing else, you should be curious about the answers you get to this question. Ask about the services offered by the career counseling center. Ask when career counseling begins. If counseling starts at the beginning of the senior year, it's too late. It should start in the first year in whatever format the school believes is best. Do you remember my advice to visit the cafeteria during your college visit? Be sure to ask the students you meet about career services at the school.

Question 38: What about Employment after Graduation?

Employment after Six Months

If the answers you receive to Question #37 are unsatisfactory, ask what the employment rate is for graduates after six months and ask what the school does to help graduates find a job after they leave school. You cannot expect any school to be totally responsible for finding you a job. However,

I do believe that every college or university in this country has a responsibility to help its students find a job even after graduation.

Question 39: Are Students Really Satisfied?

Student Satisfaction

What can you do if, you were not able to meet with current students when you visited the schools on your list? You can get student input from some guidebooks. An even better way is to speak with an admission counselor and ask to get the opinions of currently enrolled students. Are the results of student surveys available? Read carefully and read between the lines. If you can get the names of students to personally contact, do so.

If you are an international student, get a list of currently enrolled international students for each of the schools on your list. Contact them for information on their experiences. Compare the information.

Question 40: Were Graduates Happy with Their College Experience?

Alumni Satisfaction

Ask for a copy of the latest alumni satisfaction survey. Many of the college guidebooks use alumni donations as a measure of satisfaction, but I think you can find out more about the people who graduated from a school by reading recent surveys.

You can also ask for a list of the names of local alumni who have volunteered to speak with future college students. If you cannot get this information from the admission counselor, call the alumni office. If surveys of graduates are not taken and/or the information is not available to prospective students, you may want to know why.

International students should also get a list of alumni in their countries to contact for information.

Question 41: Are Parents Satisfied?

Parent Satisfaction

As long as we are asking current students and alumni to provide information on satisfaction, why not ask for a copy of the latest parent satisfaction survey? This is tricky because not many schools regularly survey parents and make the information available. Call the dean of students' office and ask for this information. I hope you get the opinions of parents because I think it's an important piece in deciding where your child should go to school. College selection is a family matter.

International parents should be given the contact information for the parents of currently enrolled students from their country.

Question 42: Why Should I Attend
This School?

Specific Reasons

Please notice the phrasing of this question. If you have asked and received information for these 42 questions, you should have a list with definite and specific reasons as to why these schools are still on your list. You should have a much clearer picture than you had before you began reading this book. This is your list, not your parents and not mine.

This is the end of Part 1. You are now finished asking questions *before* you file a single college application. Before we go to the next set of questions let me introduce you to Jack and Rosa. They are asking the same questions as you.

A TALE OF TWO STUDENTS

Jack and Rosa are completing their sopho-more year in high school and want to begin searching for colleges. Read on and let's see if you can identify with either Jack or Rosa.

Jack wants a school with large, freshman classes that is more than 500 miles away from home. Rosa wants a school with small class sizes that is close to home. Jack wants to be an engineer and several schools with good engineering programs are on his list. Rosa has no idea what she wants to study so she has several schools with strong liberal arts programs on her list. Both Jack and Rosa have selected schools in which full-time faculty teaching first-year students and each freshman is assigned an academic advisor. Jack plans to visit colleges with his parents and he will organize his visits with the admission office of each school. Rosa plans to organize her own college visit and will try to meet with faculty and current students when she is on campus. She has arranged to sit in on two classes, one freshman class and one senior-level, history class.

Both Jack and Rosa have schools on their lists with strong success rates from first to second year and with the majority of students graduating in four years. Jack is not really interested in a school's crime rate; Rosa is and has used that information to make choices. Both know the average tuition increases for the past five years for each of the schools on their lists and the average student and parent debt. The schools on Jack's list have a strong career counseling programs. Strong job placement, at the time of graduation, figures prominently on Rosa's list of schools.

Do you get the picture? Both Jack and Rosa read the 42 questions listed so far in this book and created two, different college lists, based on their preferences. That's exactly the point. If you spend the time and get answers to the questions in the PRE-APPLICATION STAGE, you are on your way to selecting the best school for you.

We are now ready to move on to the questions you should ask in the POST-ACCEPTANCE STAGE.

PART 2

POST-ACCEPTANCE STAGE

Congratulations! You have received acceptances to five schools. You would like to decide between two or three, schools, not five, so you take your investigation a bit further. The following are the questions to ask of all the schools that have sent you acceptance letters.

Question 43: What Does My Tuition Fund?

School's Budget

You may feel that asking what percentage of a school's revenue is spent on instruction, athletics, and student services is not relevant. It is. The allocation of resources is an indication of a school's priorities. I recently listened to a university president, tell a reporter on national television that the school's athletic program was the single biggest revenue source and whatever they paid the football coach was worth the money. That certainly reflects the school's priorities. The president did not elaborate on the graduation rates for athletes or how the athletic revenue was used to make the educational experience better for all students.

I realize most students and many parents will not feel comfortable phoning the president's office. If you don't want to contact the president directly, ask your admission counselor to get this information for you.

Question 44: Will I Have a Good Time?

Party School

Again, the answer to this question is an individual choice. There are several guides that will rate colleges and universities as party schools. Be careful. If party means heavy drug and alcohol use, you may want to re-consider this school. Find out if the school has a drug, alcohol, and smoking policy and compare this information with the school's crime rate.

Question 45: What about Earning College Credits in High School?

Advanced Placement Examinations

As you know, I'm a firm believer that college students should graduate in four years. There are many ways to structure your academic program so that this becomes a reality for you. One way is to enter college with college credits, and one way to do this is to take Advanced Placement (AP) courses. Most U.S. high schools offer AP exams and as you know, depending on your scores, you can be awarded college credit. First you must find out if the schools on your college list accept AP credits and if so, their criteria for awarding credit.

If you are an international student enrolled in an International Baccalaureate Program, some of your credits will also get transferred. Find out the rules from each of the schools on your list.

Question 46: How Can I Use Technology to Get College Credits in High School?

Massive Open Online Courses (MOOCs)

Another way to earn credits before entering college is to take a MOOC course. MOOCs are a type of online course with large-scale participation and open access via the web. For now they are free and for now, most don't award college credit. Some courses do carry credit and some colleges and universities are considering giving credit for specific MOOCs. The number of students taking MOOCs both in the United States and worldwide is staggering. The number of courses offered and the number of students taking the courses changes daily. That is why I am not listing statistics for high school students and adult learners, who have taken, or are taking, a MOOC course. By the time you read this, the information would be out-of-date and irrelevant.

It's worth your effort to find out if any of the schools on your list accept MOOC credits or are planning to do so in the near future. This may be one way for you to add to the number of credits you take each semester or year. The goal is to graduate in four years. Investigate any option that may assist you in reaching this goal.

Question 47: Does This School Offer Online Courses?

School Online Programs

Many high school students begin their college career in high school. More than 1.3 million high school students enrolled for college credit courses in the 2010-11 school year. That is a 67% percent increase since the last time the data was collected in 2002-03.

The majority of colleges and universities offer their own online programs, giving students the opportunity to take courses 24/7 from anywhere. This is important if you are determined to graduate in four years. You may even be allowed to take a school's online courses without being a student at the school. This can be important if you cannot get a particular course at your current school or if you need the course(s) to stay on track with your four-year graduation plan. Get a list of all online courses offered by each of the schools that is still on your list and compare.

Question 48: Is It Possible to Take Classes Online and in a Classroom?

Hybrid Programs

Technology has made it possible for online and MOOC courses to engage today's "digital native."

An online course cannot replace the in-person, classroom professor. However, some combination of in-class and online classes should be a part of the options offered by each of the schools on your list. Do you remember the "academic map" you requested in Question #11? The information from this question will help you, your academic advisor, and the registrar, plan how you can, and should, progress from freshman to senior in four years.

Question 49: Will I Go to School All Year?

Third Semester

The typical classroom is used about 40 percent of the time in a year. Semesters are about 15 weeks long. Most fall semesters begin in September and end in December. The spring semester begins in January and ends in April. This means that in the "normal" academic year, students are in classes for approximately six months. What about the other six months? What about a third semester that begins in June and ends in August?

Let me stress again that you want to graduate in four years, not five or six. If that means taking classes in the summer and taking 15 credits each semester, you should do it. What about taking on-line courses in the summer so you still can work, complete an internship, travel with your family, or participate in a community service program?

Technology has made the two-semester academic year a relic. The Ohio State University, for example, allows students to take up to three credit hours for no cost during the university's four-week May session. Beginning in 2014, the University of Iowa will allow entering students to take summer classes for free.

Create your own third semester if the school you finally choose does not have one.

Question 50: Is It Possible to Graduate in Less Than Four Years?

Graduation in Three Years

I have known several students who planned and "mapped" out their academic program to graduate in three years. These students usually had very specific reasons for accelerating their program. It can be done. For example, you could, take 18 credits a semester, attend school every summer, take online and/or MOOC courses, or get credit for an internship.

Graduating in three years, whether you are an American or international student, will save you both time and money. Not everyone can, or should, attempt to graduate in three years. However, there is no harm in asking each of the schools on your list if it is possible to graduate in less than four years.

Some schools have combined degrees. This allows students, in specific majors, to graduate in five or five and a half years with both an undergraduate and graduate degree. There are relatively few majors that allow this but I think this is a trend that will catch on in the future. The reason is technology. Please don't underestimate how creative you can be with the many technology options available today.

Let's celebrate. We are half way there with only 50 questions to go! The next set of questions is easier. That's because you have done the hardest part. Let's continue.

Question 51: May I Major in More Than One Subject?

Double Majors

There are many trends in college today and one trend is the increased number of students graduating with more than one major. These students have carefully "mapped" out their curriculum to graduate with a sufficient number of credits in each major.

Ask each of the schools on your list for the number of students who graduate with double majors. Find out the most popular combination of majors and the rules to follow. Remember to check with your academic advisor and with the registrar to be certain you are meeting all of the necessary requirements.

Question 52: How Will I Be Graded in College?

A, B, C, D Grades

I bet you have heard about grade inflation in college. Even at some of the most elite colleges and universities in the country, few students get C, D or failing grades. I know of one graduate teaching assistant who was chastised by the head of the department because she was a "tough" marker. This may seem like a dream come true to you. But there is more to the story.

Call the registrar's office for each of the schools still on your list, and ask for the grade distribution for first-semester and first-year courses. How many students in freshmen courses got a grade of D or failed courses? I will caution you that a D in a 4-credit economics course will take you several semesters of A and B grades to climb out of the hole and improve your grade point average. (Why are so many first-year students put in economics classes in the first semester? Wouldn't it be better to take it in the second year?)

Question 53: Do Freshmen Rate Professors and Courses?

Student Assessment

I think colleges and universities should be graded by their students on a regular basis. Do the schools on your list make available freshman assessment of faculty, courses, student services, etc.? Don't you think this evaluation is important? I do. How can presidents, provosts, deans, faculty, etc. know how to improve the first year experience without input from students? Rate My Professor is a popular website among college students and can provide insights into professor and course evaluations.

Maybe at this point you have eliminated another two schools from your list. Because you have done the hard work, you are now down to two or three schools and not the 20 or 25 schools on your original list. Please don't be discouraged. As I wrote earlier, this is hard work. But you are worth the time and effort.

Question 54: Who Is Talking with Students?

Communication with Students

You now have two or three schools on your list. How can you decide which of the schools will be the best fit for you and your family? Now is the time to ask different questions from the ones you asked earlier of the admission staff. If you have decided on a major, you may want to get information about the department, the faculty in your intended major, and their research projects. No question is too basic. Certainly there is no stupid question. You have the right to get this information. Notice which faculty members respond and which ones don't.

Question 55: Who Is Talking with Parents?

Communication with Parents

Your parents, or your family (if you are an adult learner), should play an important role in your college selection. This has to be a family decision because the whole family will be affected by your enrollment. So it's important that the chosen school is a good fit for everyone involved. The best schools have been communicating with parents since the time of application. After acceptance, communication from the president, provost, chief financial officer, career counselor, etc., should continue. Parents have a responsibility to get connected with the person(s) who can provide feedback. Parents' questions may center on payment options or loan re-payment plans. They should get the facts now and not wait until after enrollment to ask.

Question 56: How Can I Get Unfiltered Information?

Current Students

In Question # 8, I suggested that instead of taking the standard admission tour when visiting schools, you opt to eat in the cafeteria and ask students for their opinions of the school. Now it is even more important to get student input. Try to identify students you know who are attending the schools still on your list. Ask them to give you their honest assessment of the school's curriculum, faculty, student services, career services and anything else that is important to you. This unfiltered information could be a game changer for you. If the information you receive from current students is different from published information, contact the admission counselor with your concerns.

If you are an international student, it will be more difficult, but not impossible, to get this information. I urge you to contact current students in the most convenient way for you.

Question 57: How Can My Parents Get Unfiltered Information?

Current Parents

Let's not underestimate the importance of input from the parents of domestic and international students to the parents of future college students. As with Question # 56, this unfiltered information can point the family in the direction of one school over another. Don't just accept the endorsements in a view book or on the website. Ask for the names of parents whose son or daughter is currently enrolled. Compare the information you get from parents with the published information. There should be a match between the two.

Question 58: How Can I Have a Conversation with Graduates?

Alumni

Both prospective students and parents should have conversations with graduates of the schools still on their list. Many schools have regional alumni representatives who meet with prospective families. (Some may Skype!) This interaction is valuable and can be informative but please remember that these are volunteers. They had a great experience or they would not be alumni representatives.

Try to locate graduates who are not in the volunteer program and get their unfiltered advice on the merits of the schools. No school is perfect and there will always be some unhappy graduates. Just be sure that no "red flags" are raised by the information you receive from alumni.

Question 59: What If I Need Counseling?

Counseling Services

There are many students who start school with mental health, eating disorders or other emotional problems and the demands of the first year often worsen those problems. Every school should have a psychological counseling center, a place where stressed students can get information and assistance. There is nothing wrong with seeking help and nothing wrong with asking for information about available counseling services. Please don't assume that you will never need help. I cannot tell you of the number of parents and students I advised who had no idea how to get counseling assistance. Get the information now in case you need it later on.

Question 60: What If I Have a Disability?

Disability Services

Federal law requires colleges and universities to provide disabled students with appropriate services. What if you are deaf or blind? What if you have been diagnosed with an attention deficit disorder? What are the services offered by the remaining schools on your list? Get the information now if you are a disabled person and compare the services. Contact the office that handles disabled students, and make certain that the information you receive from the staff matches what is publicized on the website or in the school catalog.

Question 61: Is It Possible to Follow My Exercise and Eating Programs?

Health and Wellness Programs

Maybe having a well-equipped gym or healthy meal choices is not important to you. It is for some people. I remember hearing in high school that many freshmen gained 15 pounds in their first year. I did and it took me until the end of sophomore year to lose the weight I gained. You will want and need to take a break from studying. You should have some sport or exercise program that you can make part of your day. Maybe you want to take a meditation or yoga class?

You should be able to eat balanced meals and get something to eat at midnight other than pizza, when you're studying for an exam or finishing a term paper. If you have food allergies, you should be able to follow your prescribed diet.

These issues may not be deal breakers, but they should be considered when making your final choice. Compare the wellness programs of the schools on your list and decide for yourself how this information factors into your final decision.

International students may want to know if they will be able to get some of the foods they eat at home, either on campus or in local restaurants.

Question 62: What Happens If I Get Sick or Have An Accident?

Emergency Programs

Every school should have an emergency program. How are parents notified of an emergency? What is the closest affiliated hospital? These questions may not seem important to you now. After enrollment, you, and your family, will want to know what procedures are in place in case something happens to you. Get information from the Heath Center staff or whatever office administers this program.

Question 63: Who Can I Call?

Important Contacts

By this time you should have a list of the names and numbers of important administrators and faculty. You should have contact information for the following: admission office, financial aid office, academic dean's office, dean of students' office, first-year advisor, registrar, career counselor, counseling director, bursar, residence hall directors, head of police services, and alumni office. Both students and parents should have this list. You will add some names and subtract others after you enroll. You probably should have the name and contact information for the school's president, just in case you need it.

Question 64: What Is It Like to Live on Campus?

Residence Halls

Some of you reading this book may decide that you want to save money and commute to school from home. Just 30 percent of all beginning college students live on campus. There is nothing wrong with that decision. I was a commuter student. I received an excellent education and I learned the value of managing my time well. It may surprise you to learn that the majority of college and university students commute to school. However, if you decide that you want to live on campus that is your decision. Remember it will add to your college expenses.

There are as many residence life programs as there are schools with residence halls. You have to decide what is important to you. Would you prefer co-educational dorms or would you rather have same-sex dorms? What amenities are important to you? Will you be allowed to decorate your room? Are the residencies opened during holidays, between semesters and in the summer?

Find out the rules and regulations for living on campus. Ask for the percentage of students living on-campus. That percentage will give you some idea of campus life. Find out if you have to live on campus for all four years. Find out how and when dormitory rooms are assigned and if it's possible to change your room.

If you are an international student, ask for the percentage of international students who live on campus. Also find out if a school's policy is to assign international students to room with other international students or with American students. This is a matter of preference but I recommend trying to room with someone who is not from your country. You will have a very different college experience if you have an American roommate.

Question 65: What If I Don't Want to Live on Campus?

Off-Campus Housing

Some schools cannot accommodate all of the students who want to live on campus and provide off-campus housing options. This may be something you want to consider. In general, living off-campus is cheaper than on campus. Depending on which part of the country you live in, rents can be nego-tiated and less-expensive meals made. If you are thinking about living off-campus as a way to save money, speak with the person in charge of placing students in apartments or houses and make this a part of your financial calculations.

Question 66: Where Do I Live When the Semester Is Over?

Holiday and Summer Living Arrangements

I knew many families who discovered, as one se-mester ended and before another one began, that the residence halls were not open during holidays or between semesters. Some schools charge a fee to stay in dormitories during off periods. That means more money and unhappy customers. Find out the options, especially if there is a long dis-tance between your home and your school. If you plan to take classes in the summer, find out if on-campus living is available. Some schools renovate their residence halls during the summer months or rent their dormitory rooms to high school stu-dents or students from other countries for summer programs.

The answer to this question is especially important for international students who do not travel home for most U.S. holidays.

———————•———————

Question 67: Do I Have a Choice of Who I Live With?

Roommates

You can probably imagine how difficult it will be if you are assigned a roommate and the two of you just can't get along. This happened to one of my daughters and nearly sabotaged her first semester. I really urge you to get ahead of this situation. Many students arrive on campus never knowing what it means to share a room. Find out what your options are. Are freshmen assigned one, two, three or four roommates? Is there overcrowding on the campus? A bad living arrangement can contribute to making you a transfer statistic. Your living arrangement, along with your academic program, is part of the collegiate experience. It should be as pleasant as possible.

International students please reread my suggestions in Question #64.

Question 68: Is There Life After Classes?

Clubs and Organizations

If you believe, as I do, that you need to have a life outside of the classroom, then a list of clubs and campus organizations is important information. Think about the extracurricular activities important to you now and whether you want to pursue them in college. Ask yourself the question: what would I like to do when I am not in class, taking an online course, or studying? Decide if the schools still on your list match your interests. One final thought: find out the percentage of students who join clubs and organizations. That information will give you some insight into the vitality of this part of the school's student-service program.

International students should ask if there is an international student organization and, if so, what activities are sponsored by the club.

Question 69: May I Take Classes Abroad?
Study Abroad Opportunities

I really think you should study abroad. Not for two weeks, in between semesters, or for a month after a semester ends, but at least for one semester. Ideally, the "junior year abroad" program of past is the best model. I realize most students have neither the time nor the money to study abroad for one year. For students in specific majors, like the sciences, it may even jeopardize graduating in four years.

Still, I think the benefits of studying abroad outweigh the negatives. You will not be the same person after a semester abroad that you were before. You will view the world in different ways. You will mature and gain confidence. You will make new friends, learn a new language and see a different part of the world. This is part of being educated.

Learn all of the study abroad opportunities at the schools on your list. Compute additional costs into your family's financing plan if you decide to study abroad.

A word of caution: be sure to meet with your academic advisor so that all of the courses you take when studying abroad will transfer and count toward your graduation requirements. When you go abroad, bring a hard copy of the approved courses with you, and leave a hard copy at home with your parents as a safety precaution. You don't want any surprises when you return from your study abroad experience.

Question 70: Is It Possible to Play a Sport in College?

Athletics

The importance of athletics in your college decision is a personal choice. Most college students will not make the varsity team or be awarded full, athletic scholarships. Maybe you have an interest in sports, not as a participant, but as a spectator. You like the idea of football and basketball games as an opportunity to unwind from studying and term papers. Examine the athletic opportunities in your final schools and compare the programs.

Question 71: May I Practice My Faith in College?

Religious Observance

It is important, for some students, to be able to practice their religious beliefs. If this is true for you, review the websites of each of the remaining schools on your list. Is there an interfaith center? Compare the services of the campus ministry offices.

International students will want to know how their religious holidays are observed on campus.

———•———

Let's check in with Jack and Rosa. They have read all of these 71 questions and received answers to most of them. Jack would not mind enrolling in a party school. He likes the idea of joining a fraternity. Rosa does not want a party school. At this stage in her life, Rosa is interested in pursuing her individual interests and meeting students who are different, from her. Jack plans to enroll in a MOOC course that is approved by both of the final schools on his list. Rosa is taking two AP classes and expects to have the courses accepted by the schools on her list.

Jack definitely wants a Division I school with a large athletic program. Rosa is content

> *with a Division III school. Jack convinces his parents that it will be cheaper to live off-campus and he finds three other first- year students who want to share a house with him. Rosa, and her parents, wants the security of a residence hall. Both Rosa and Jack definitely want to study abroad for a semester and are comparing the options of their final schools.*

If you have done the work suggested in this book up to now, a clear "winner" will surface. You will know where you should enroll and why. The 71 questions have given you a roadmap to help you make your final decision. This is what happened for Jack and Rosa and for their families. They did the work and spent the time to make the best, informed choice.

It's May 1st and the date most schools require a deposit to hold a place in the freshman class. Usually the deposit is non-refundable. That is not a problem for Jack or Rosa or you. You know you have chosen the best school for you and your family.

Now let's examine some of the questions you should ask from the time that deposit is made until the time you begin classes. Relax. The worst is over.

Question 72: What Happens After May 1ˢᵗ?

Post Deposit

Once your deposit is received by the admission office, you will get information from the dean of students, the staff from the residence life program, the registrar, the bursar and your academic dean. Depending on prior communication, you will receive information from the athletics office staff or the president of the student government association. Keep everything you receive in a file folder. Parents should also keep their own portfolio of information.

Question 73: What Happens During Orientation?

Student Orientation

Every school has an orientation program. Some are held in June after high school graduation. Some are held in August just before school begins. Most of the programs, in my opinion, cram too much information in too little time. I have seen many students with crazed looks on their faces after one day of orientation. A number of administrators and staff make presentations. Their information is very important. But it is too much information. (Since you read this book, you already have a great deal of information that is typically given at orientation.)

Be aware that many orientation programs also include testing in math and/or English. Programs
can be as short as two days or as long as a week.
Make sure you get the dates for orientation as
soon as you send in your deposit. You want to be
certain that there is no conflict with your current
school or work schedule, or work schedule if you
are an adult learner. You may be able to meet your
roommate, or find your first-year advisor during
orientation.

Attending a June orientation is particularly difficult for international students and for other students who need to travel long distances. Find out
if the school has an online orientation program and
sign up for the later August or September program
if you cannot make it to campus in June.

Question 74: Is There an Orientation Program for Parents?

Parent Orientation

There was a time in my administrative career when I was able to organize two orientation programs: one for students and one for parents. Many schools invite parents to campus at the same time students are on campus for orientation. I think the orientations should be separate because parents will have different questions from students.

Question 75: What Courses Will I Take in the First Semester?

Registration

Throughout this book, I have stressed, the importance of establishing a good relationship with the registrar's office staff from the very beginning of your academic career. Someone, in that office, will determine if, and when, you graduate. Find out if registration is part of your orientation program, and follow the rules for registration carefully. Most schools assign general education courses to first-year students. These are the courses that are needed by all majors to graduate. You can expect to study English and math in your first semester.

Many registrar's offices are contained within a customer service or advising area. Be sure to locate this office and connect with someone who can provide you with information on course sequencing, graduation requirements, etc.

You know from previous questions that you may want to add a course to your schedule. You may want to substitute the economics class for another course. You may want to adjust your schedule so that you do not have four-hour breaks between classes. This is the time to get your first-semester class schedule nailed down. If you are certain about the major you want to study, you should be given an "academic road map" of the courses needed for graduation and the proper sequencing of those courses.

Over the years I have seen hundreds of students placed on academic probation. When evaluating their transcripts, I noticed that these students were often improperly enrolled in courses. They could not successfully complete the second course because they had not yet studied the first one. The result was a low or failing grade. I don't want that to happen to you. Follow your "academic road map."

Question 76: What Is My "Academic Bible"?

Catalog

I strongly suggest that you and your parents to get a hard copy of the catalog for the year you enter school. Many colleges and universities will not give you a hard copy unless you ask for it. I know everything is online today but I also know that academic rules and regulations change. The catalog serves as a record of the rules that were in place the year you entered school. I have seen many graduation discrepancies cleared up after officials reviewed the catalog. Make sure you stop by the registrar's office to get your copy, preferably during orientation.

Question 77: May I Use My Smartphone or Tablet in Class?

Classroom Rules

Even though most professors no longer take attendance, many do not look favorably on students who are frequently absent from their classes. They are also not thrilled with students who sit in the back of the room constantly texting friends. Find out what electronic devices are acceptable in each class.

You have done a good job of selecting the best school for you. Get the most out of the experience.

Arrive in class on time and well prepared. Don't ask for extra time to complete a class assignment or turn in a term paper. Do ask for extra help if you think you need it. Your professors have scheduled office hours. Make an appointment to discuss any problems you are having in class. Be sure you understand clearly how final grades are determined. You don't want any surprises at the end of the semester.

Question 78: What Happens If I Have to Leave School?

Leave of Absence

Things happen. Some students get sick or have to return home because some member of the family is sick. Some adult learners change jobs and cannot juggle the demands of a new job and school at the same time. Some families cannot meet tuition payments. You already have the names and contact information for your first-year academic advisor, registrar, bursar and financial aid counselor. If for some reason you need to take a leave of absence, be sure you understand the rules for officially withdrawing from school, and at the same time, find out the process for re-admission.

If you receive federal or state financial aid and need to leave school, there may be consequences.

Don't be surprised if you start receiving notices to begin re-paying your student loans. Get all of this sorted out before you leave school. You already have the names and contact information for you first-year academic advisor, registrar, bursar and financial aid counselor. Contact each of them if you have to leave school.

If you do have to leave school, maybe you can take an online course or an approved MOOC? Why not? Technology has made it possible for you to continue with your studies even if you cannot be physically present on campus.

Question 79: When Does School Start and Stop?

Four-Year Calendar

Request a four-year calendar of semester start and stop dates so your parents can schedule trips to school and you can plan for family vacations or trips home. Even "approximate" dates will allow for better planning. Try to get this information from your school. It will help everyone in the family in the future.

Question 80: Do I Need a Doctor's Note
to Begin School?

Health Regulations

Federal and state laws require college and university students to have specific immunizations. The required "shots" may vary from state to state. Be sure you meet the health regulations of the state of your school. This is not a trivial matter. I knew many students who did not have the required immunizations and when the time came to pre-register for the second semester, a hold was put on their registration until they could show proof of their immunizations. In many cases, by the time the immunization record was submitted, some of the classes the students wanted were closed. This is not a great way to start your second semester. Keep accurate records of your immunizations. Parents should also have a copy of your immunization form.

Intenational students are also required to enter the U.S. with all of the required immunizations.

-----•-----

Question 81: What Happens If Parents Lose Their Jobs?

Change in Family Finances

Perhaps you received a good financial aid package from your chosen school, and this was one of the reasons you selected the school. You and your family calculated that through some combination of savings, aid, (federal, state and school), loans, and work, you could afford to attend this college. Maybe the financial calculations you made a few months ago are no longer accurate? What happens if your family's finances change? What if one, or both of your parents, lose their jobs or are denied the parent loan they were counting on to help finance your education? Notify your financial aid counselor immediately if your family's financial circumstances change. Explain the situation. Maybe the counselor will increase your loan or grant amount? Maybe you will need, to commute from home until your family's financial situation improves? Don't panic. Be honest and open with your financial aid counselor. In most situations, the school will help you solve your financial problems.

Question 82: May I Pay My Tuition in Installments?

Payment Plans and Financing Options

Because you have read and followed the suggestions in this book, you already know the various payment options available to you and your family. If your financial circumstances change, you may wish to re-visit these options. Many colleges and universities do not require full tuition payment at the beginning of a semester. Maybe you can work out a monthly payment plan with the bursar? Remember you are the customer. Your school will work with you to help you to stay in school and meet your financial obligations. Both you and your school want you to graduate in four years!

Question 83: Should I Get a Job in College?

Employment

You have probably guessed that I am a big fan of students working in college. I think it is reasonable to suggest that you can take 15 credits and work 10 to 20 hours a week. There is a great deal of research to suggest that students who work have better time-management skills and get better grades than those who don't. Your college part-time job might even become a full-time job after graduation, as was the case for me.

Many schools now also offer cooperative education programs that allow students to study for a semester and then work for a semester. I think this is a valuable option.

If the money you earn is not needed to pay for tuition or books, use it to pay for your day-to-day living expenses. Create a budget and stick to it. This is a good lesson to learn for later in life.

Question 84: Do I Have to Complete All My High School Courses?

"Senioritis"

It happens to a lot of high school students. You are accepted to the college of your choice and decide to take it easy for the last semester of high school.

Don't do it. Remember your acceptance is based on the information you gave the admission office at the time you applied. Admission counselors do check to be sure you completed the high school courses you listed. I have known students who had to attend summer school because they failed a senior course and their college would not admit them until all of the entrance requirements were met.

Question 85: Should I Get a Car?

First Semester and "Wheels"

This question is probably more for parents than students. I strongly recommend that students do not have a car the first semester of college. There are just too many temptations when you are the student with "wheels". It's easy for friends to take advantage of you, your car and your time. In particular, you really don't need a car if you live on campus. This is different, of course, for commuter students. You will need a car if public transportation is not available. Find out if first-year students are given parking spaces. You don't want to spend 30 minutes looking for a space to park your car and be late for class.

Question 86: Is It Normal to Feel Homesick?

Homesick

It happens to many students. After the first few weeks of school, the newness wears off and homesickness kicks in. This is normal and nothing to worry about. If you are troubled, make an appointment to meet with a counselor and discuss your problems. Most schools plan parents' week-ends in October for just this reason. You can re-connect with your family, and maybe even get a few home cooked meals. Another stressful time in the first semester is around the Thanksgiving holiday in November. Many students travel home and realize that they are no longer the person they were when they left in August. This too, is normal. You are not the same person.

You know term papers are due soon and you have five final exams. Remember you have been meeting frequently with your academic advisor and course professors. You have some idea of your grades going into the final examinations. Enjoy the holiday and the time with family and friends.

Question 87: Is It Normal to Miss My Child?

Empty Nest

Most parents experience withdrawal when their child, especially if it is their first one, leaves for college. This is a natural reaction to the dramatic shift in the family dynamic. If you are an adult learner, returning to school after many years, your family life will also change. If you are a parent, know that the empty nest feelings will pass. You may even welcome the peace and quiet that comes with having a child 200 miles away from home or in another country. That also is a normal feeling that will pass. But life will never be the same. This rite of passage is permanent.

If you are an adult learner returning to school after many years, your family life will also change. No longer will you have as much time to spend with your wife or husband and children. College is an adjustment for everyone.

Question 88: Should I Work Even If I don't Get Paid?

Internships

Most high school graduates want to work in the summer before starting college but summer jobs are often difficult to get. If that is the case for you, apply for an internship, even if it is unpaid. I am a big supporter of internship programs and know of many students who successfully moved from an internship to a job. Volunteer. Network with family and friends. Do whatever it takes to do *something* in the summer before starting college.

Let's get back to Jack and Rosa. Both of these students are happy with their college choice. They did enroll in the best school for each of them, although the schools are very different. They both successfully navigated the often troublesome first-year waters, and both have grade point averages over 3.0. Jack did join a fraternity and Rosa did join the debate team. They both studied abroad at the beginning of their junior year. They are on track to graduate in four years. At the end of junior year, Jack had a $10,000 loan bill and his parents owed another $10,000. Rosa's loan bill is $12,000 and her parents so far owe $15,000. It was important to both Rosa and her parents that she live on campus even though that increased expenses. Jack met frequently with his academic advisor and with the staff in the career counseling office. He believes his engineering degree and two internships will help him when he applies for a job.

Rosa will graduate with a degree in modern foreign languages. She would like to work abroad using her language skills. She has met frequently with the staff in the career counseling center and with her academic advisor. The alumni office has identified an alumnus, who lives in Italy, willing to help Rosa find a job.

Both Jack and Rosa are ready to begin their senior and final year of college.

Question 89: How Can I Prepare for Job Interviews?

Company Interviews

Make certain that you have a list of the dates and times for all campus visits by company recruiters. Your school should have done a great job of preparing you for interviews. You began working with the staff in the career counseling office since your freshman year. You resume is impressive. All of your internships are listed on your transcript as are all of the MOOC courses you took over the past three years. The college you attended during your study abroad semester is listed. You have four excellent references. Your grade point average, at the end of your junior year, is 3.40.

You have participated in mock interviews and you even bought an interview "outfit."

Meet with as many company representatives as possible. Hone your interviewing skills, and get feedback from the company representatives whenever possible.

Question 90: How Much Debt Is Too Much Debt?

Debt Ratios and Starting Salaries

Maybe you were already offered a job during one of the company interviews? The starting salary of $40,000 is reasonable. But when you calculate your monthly loan payment and your take-home pay, you are uncomfortable with your remaining income. I read on one federal website that an acceptable debt-to-starting-salary ratio is no more than 15 percent. That means that you want to be certain you are paying no more than 15 percent of your starting salary to service your student loan bill.

I'm sure you have read or heard about college graduates living in their parents' basements because, although they have a job, they are not earning enough to have their own apartment. That's not for you. You still have one year to change this financial situation. You have had the same financial aid counselor for the past three years. She knows you and your finances. Make an appointment to discuss the situation. Can your grant aid be increased? Can you increase the number of hours you work? Can you re-adjust your budget? Many financial aid offices have on staff, or can make available, financial experts who can help you plan this next phase of your college financing plan. Find out if your school's financial aid office participates in SALT, an on-line financial literacy program which includes money management strategies for budgeting, credit cards and banking.

Question 91: Is It OK to Go to Graduate School Right After College?

Graduate Schools

You may decide that you don't want to go to work right after graduation. Maybe you are considering graduate school? Some of the same principles outlined in this book for undergraduates would also apply to graduate school selection and admission. Many graduate students are sponsored, meaning they pay little or no tuition. Some graduate students receive a stipend to live while in graduate school. Sometimes graduate students are required to teach undergraduate students or assist faculty with research projects. You should get all this information before making a final decision. You already know, because you asked before you even applied, about your school's track record for graduate school acceptance.

Question 92: Is It OK to Go to Professional School Right After College?

Professional Schools

If you are a pre-medical or pre-dental student, you already know the acceptance rate of your college to medical and dental schools. The same is true of law, pharmacy, etc. You probably won't get any "free" financial aid to attend professional school, and this is where the loan bill can really balloon. Compare what you estimate you will need to borrow with what you can reasonably expect to earn after graduation. Seek the advice of a professional expert or a certified financial planner, if necessary. No, it is not too early to consider this. There are many doctors, dentists and lawyers with exorbitant loan bills. You don't want to start your career with unmanageable financial obligations. As discussed in Question #9, debt is manageable or unmanageable in relation to your salary.

Question 93: How Can I Stay Connected to My School After Graduation?

Free Courses

Many graduates complain that the first time they hear from their school is to ask for money. This is not a good way to begin a post-graduation relationship. Some schools do things differently. For example, some colleges and universities, give graduating students a certificate to take one free course, either online or on campus. That keeps the graduate engaged and sends a positive message.

Question 94   Who Do I Communicate with After Graduation?

Alumni Office

Before you leave college, pay a visit to the alumni office. Get a list of alumni in your area and a list of graduates who have volunteered to help young alumni with networking opportunities or internships. Do this before you leave school. It is much more difficult to do once you are no longer on campus.

This is the end of Part 2. Now we move to the time after you graduate.

PART 3

POST-GRADUATION STAGE

Bravo! You have successfully graduated. Now what happens? Does your relationship with your college or university end when you walk across the stage at graduation? It should not. We are about to enter the POST-GRADUATION STAGE of this book. We are almost done.

Question 95: Employed, Unemployed, or Underemployed?

Jobs at Graduation

You can accuse me of repeating a question. I would agree that Question # 37 asked this question. But the information you received is four years old and I am betting that the statistics have changed because colleges are paying more attention to career counseling and jobs. So ask it again. How many graduates have jobs as they leave school and what are the starting salaries, by major, of recent graduates? Are they employed or underemployed? You know from reading this book that a job after graduation is one of the primary criteria in college choice.

Question 96: Employed, Unemployed, or Underemployed After Six Months?

Jobs after Six Months

I am guilty again. Question #38 also asks this question. I have the same rationale for repeating this question as I did for the previous one. It's four years later. Let's fast forward to six months after graduation. Are you living at home in your parents' basement? Are you spending your days applying to any job, regardless of your qualifications? There are positive things you can do to look for the kind of job you want. The first is to network as much as possible. If you can afford it, volunteer or sign up for an unpaid internship. Don't get discouraged and don't give up. Get up and get out every day. Stay connected with the career counseling staff of your school. Be persistent. Be positive. Be persuasive.

Question 97: May I Contact Alumni to Help Me Find a Job?

Alumni Connections

Before you left college you were given a list of alumni in your area. Contact the graduates on your list for assistance. Get a list of all of the alumni clubs in your area or region. Consider joining the club. That is a great way to network. Most people, I believe, find jobs through contacts. I have seen this happen with so many students and in my own family. Stay connected to your school by becoming an active member of the alumni association. That membership may prove beneficial to you as you enter the job market or change jobs.

Question 98: Will I Hear from Someone in My Graduating Class?

Class Agents

Class agents are people who have volunteered to communicate with you after graduation. You should have the name and contact information of your class agent(s). Get in touch. It's a great way to stay connected with your classmates and with your school. It's important for many reasons to continue your relationship with your school after graduation. Remember you had a great time in college. You had good experiences and have good memories. Stay connected with your class agents or consider becoming an agent yourself.

Question 99: How Will My School Stay Connected to Me After Graduation?

School Connections

It's not only your responsibility to stay connected. Your school has an obligation to stay connected to its graduates. You should continue to receive information and bulletins from your college or university on a regular basis. You should receive a list of courses you could take online either free or at a discounted rate. Many colleges and universities make online courses available in perpetuity. It may be fun to watch a lecture you took in your junior year. Technology has made it possible to stay connected as much or as little as you want.

Your college or university should communicate with you its recent awards or distinctions. I am not only referring to your school's ranking. You should know how many merit scholars enrolled last semester. You should know how many Fulbright scholarships were awarded. You should know if one of your school's graduates has distinguished himself or herself. The communication that began before you even applied should continue after graduation. That is customer service. That is the way it should be.

> *Are you curious to know what happened to Jack and Rosa after graduation? Jack graduated with an engineering degree. He started a job at $70,000 but needed to re-locate. Jack's parents weren't too happy about this, but it was a good job and in a part of the country they look forward to visiting. Jack continues to take MOOC courses and online courses from his "alma mater."*
>
> *Rosa is living in Italy. She is a translator for a company and earns $50,000 a year. She plans to return home after two years and enroll in graduate school. Rosa stays connected with her college through the alumni chapter of her school in Italy. Both Jack and Rosa contribute to their schools. Both want to give back because they had such good experiences. They did the hard work all those many years ago and chose the right schools for them.*
>
> *The same will be true for you.*

Question 100: Is There Anything More
I Need to Find Out?

Getting Answers

I am leaving this last question for you to answer. Do you feel after reading these questions, that you have the tools to select the best college or university for you? Were the questions listed and the information presented helpful? Did you learn more about yourself as a person by answering some of these questions? Were you disappointed that you did not, or could not, get answers to many of the questions from the schools on your original list?

This is not the end of this book. I am now going to show you how to organize your questions and who to contact to have your questions answered. How you communicate is up to you. Maybe you prefer email or texting? Maybe you would like to speak with a real person? Maybe you want to Skype? It's up to you.

Use the chart in the next section to help you find the answers to all the questions in this book. It will show you where to look or who to contact for information. Try to spend one hour a week, for a year if you can, pulling all of the information together before you apply to college. If you don't have a year left before you begin your college search, then you will need to spend more than an hour a week. Please remember that if you follow the guidelines in this book *you cannot fail*. You will successfully identify the best school for you and for your family and one that you can afford.

CONCLUSION

You can do this. No matter your age, background, grades, income, or where you live, there is a college or university for you and one you can afford. Don't listen to all of the negatives about college admission and financial aid. Don't get discouraged. Think about selecting a college as an adventure, one that will allow you to discover new aspects about yourself and one that can be an enjoyable experience.

This is the end of our journey together but just the beginning of your college journey.

The day after I finished writing this book, I attended a family gathering. One of my relatives expressed concern about her 16-year old son and the anxiety the family had about finding the right college for him. So I gave Hana's son, Andy a copy of this book. He read it and told me the following: "I believe this book asks many questions I never

would have asked. After reading it I realize that college is not just for the wealthy, fortunate or upper class. This book is the key to my future."

I hope the information in this book will also be the key to your future.

THE RIGHT QUESTIONS

On the following pages are the 100 questions from this book, with suggestions for finding the information you need. Use this chart to help you ask the right questions at each stage—and get the answers.

PART 1: PRE-APPLICATION STAGE		
Question	Topic	How to Get Answers
1: Where Do I Want to Go to School?	School Location and Size	Buy a guidebook, and begin to build a list of schools based on your personal preferences.
2: Do I Want to Go to a College or a University?	Type of School	Use the guidebook to continue to build a list of schools based on your personal preferences.
3: Do I Know What I Want to Study?	College and University Majors	If you have not decided on a specific major, consider adding some liberal arts to your list.

4: Am I a Good Student?	Honors Program	Take a look at the schools on your list so far, and check their websites for information about honors programs.
5: What Are Students Studying?	Most Popular Majors	Review the information in the guidebook. Then contact the admission office of each school on your list for additional information.
6: Will I Meet Students from Other Parts of the United States and World?	Diversity	This is a personal preference, and the guidebook should provide all the information you need to answer this question.

Question	Topic	How to Get Answers
7: How Is Big for First-Year Students?	Average Class Size	Contact the admission office of each school on your list to get information on the average class size for first-year courses.
8: Who Will Teach Me?	Full-time Faculty, Adjunct Faculty, and Graduate Assistants	Review the guidebook, and contact the academic dean's office of each school on your list.
9: May I Sit in on Classes Before I Apply?	Classroom Visit	Create your own campus visit to include sitting in on two classes.

10: How Many Freshmen Become Sophomores?	Progression and Graduation	Contact the academic dean's office or the office for retention services.
11: How Long Will It Take Me to Graduate?	Graduation in Four, Five, and Six Years	Contact the academic dean's office or the office for retention services.
12: How Many Credits Do I Need to Graduate?	Graduation Credits	Call the registrar's office for this important information; this number will influence your entire academic career.
13: Do I Have Research Interests?	Research with Faculty	Contact the department chairperson or the academic dean to get this information.

Question	Topic	How to Get Answers
14: How Can I Manage Classes in the First Year?	Academic Support Services	Contact the academic dean's office or the office of retention services.
15: What Are My Interests?	Student Services	Contact the dean of students' office for this information.
16: Who Is Talking with Me?	Communication with Students	Get the answer to this question from an admission counselor.
17: Who Is Talking with Parents?	Communication with Parents	Get a list of parents from the admission office.

18: How Safe Are the Schools on My List?	Crime Rate	Contact the security office for details.
19: Why Should I Attend Your School?	Specific Reasons	Contact the dean's office and the admission office to be certain their answers to this question match.
20: Why Are Students Leaving?	Transferring Out	The schools still on your list may have a transfer counselor in the admission office.
21: Why Are Students Enrolling?	Transferring In	Contact the transfer counselor if there is one.

Question	Topic	How to Get Answers
22: Will I Fit In?	The Typical Student	Review the information in your guidebook, and contact the admission office to get their answer to this question.
23: Will I Graduate?	Profile of Students Who Graduate	Check with the office that handles student services and retention to get the answer to this question.
24: What About Advanced Degrees?	Graduate- and Professional- School Placement	Contact the academic dean's office or specific department.

25: Can I Afford This School?	Tuition Increases	Contact the bursar's office for information.
26: Are There Other Costs Besides Tuition?	Other Costs	Contact the financial aid office to get the answer.
27: What Kind of Financial Aid is Available?	Average Financial Aid Package	Contact the financial aid office.
28: Are There Tools to Help Me Calculate the Total Cost of Attendance?	Net Price Calculators	Check the website for each school on your list.

Question	Topic	How to Get Answers
29: Will I Receive the Same Amount of Financial Aid Each Year I Am in School?	Bait and Switch	The financial aid office should answer this question.
30: Will I Have to Pay Full Tuition?	Sticker Shock	Review the rules for scholarships and grants, and then contact someone in the admission and financial aid offices to further explain.

31: Does Everyone Get Financial Aid?	Percentages on Aid	Check with the financial aid office for the most recent percentages of students on aid.
32: Will I Have to Take Out Loans for College?	Student Debt	Contact the financial aid office for the most recent debt figures.
33: Will My Parents Have to Take Out Loans?	Parent Debt	Contact the financial aid office for the most recent debt figures.
34: How Do I Know If I Am Borrowing Too Much?	Loan Limits and Starting Salaries	Contact the financial aid office for this information.

Question	Topic	How to Get Answers
35: Is There Some Way to Reduce My Loan Bill?	Loan Forgiveness Programs	Either the admission office or financial aid office can answer this question.
36: Is It Possible to See Samples of Financial Aid Award Letters?	Online Financial-Aid Award Letters	Ask the financial aid office for sample letters.
37: Who Can Help Me Find a Job?	Career Counseling	Check with the career counseling office for all of its services from first through fourth year.

38: What About Employment After Graduation?	Employment After Six Months	Check with the career counseling office for all of its services from first through fourth year.
39: Are Students Really Satisfied?	Student Satisfaction	Contact the dean of students' office for this information.
40: Were Graduates Happy with Their College Experience?	Alumni Satisfaction	Contact the alumni office.
41: Are Parents Satisfied?	Parent Satisfaction	Contact the dean of students' office.
42: Why Should I Attend This School?	Specific Reasons	If you don't already know the answer, review what you have learned from asking the previous questions.

PART 2: POST-ACCEPTANCE STAGE		
Question	Topic	How to Get Answers
43: What Does My Tuition Fund?	School's Budget	You may need to contact the president's office for an answer to this question.
44: Will I Have a Good Time?	Party School	Review the information in your guidebook, and verify with currently enrolled students.
45: What About Earning College Credits in High School?	Advanced Placement Exams	Contact the admission office for help with this question.

46: How Can I Use Technology to Get College Credits in High School?	Massive Open Online Courses (MOOCs)	Contact the academic dean's office for guidance about MOOCs.
47: Does This School Offer Online Courses?	School Online Programs	Review the website of each school still on your list.
48: Is It Possible to Take Classes Online *and* in a Classroom?	Hybrid Programs	Review each school's website, and verify the information with the academic dean's office.
49: Will I Go to School All Year?	Third Semester	Contact the academic dean's office for this information.

Question	Topic	How to Get Answers
50: Is It Possible to Graduate in Less Than Four Years?	Graduation in Three Years	Check with the academic dean's office.
51: May I Major in More Than One Subject?	Double Majors	Check with the academic dean's office.
52: How Will I Be Graded in College?	A, B, C, D Grades	Check with the academic dean's office.
53: Do Freshmen Rate Professors and Courses?	Assessment	If this information is not online, contact the academic dean's office.

54: Who Is Talking with Students?	Communication with Students	Contact the academic dean's office and individual departments for more information.
55: Who Is Talking with Parents?	Communication with Parents	Contact the admission office for this information.
56: How Can I Get Unfiltered Communication?	Current Students	Either the admission office or the dean of students' office should provide the names of students you can contact.
57: How Can My Parents Get Unfiltered Communication?	Current Parents	Either the admission office or the dean of students' office should provide the names of parents to contact.

Question	Topic	How to Get Answers
58: How Can I Have a Conversation with Graduates?	Alumni	Contact the alumni office for this information.
59: What If I Need Counseling?	Psychological Counseling Services	Contact the office responsible for these services that is listed on the website, and ask for a complete list of services.
60: What If I Have a Disability?	Disability Services	Contact the office responsible for these services that is listed on the website, and ask for a complete list of services.

61: Is It Possible to Follow My Exercise and Eating Programs?	Health and Wellness Programs	Contact the dean of student's office.
62: What Happens If I Get Sick or Have an Accident?	Emergency Programs	The responsibility for this program will vary from school to school. Review the website for the specific office location for each of the schools on your list.
63: Who Can I Call?	Important Contacts	By now, you probably have your own list. Add any additional information from the website and catalog.

Question	Topic	How to Get Answers
64: What Is It Like to Live on Campus?	Residence Halls	Contact the residential-life office as a starting place.
65: What If I Don't Want to Live on Campus?	Off-Campus Housing	Check with the residential-life office.
66: Where Do I Live When the Semester Is Over?	Holiday and Summer Living Arrangements	Check with the residential-life office.
67: Do I Have a Choice of Who I Live With?	Roommates	Check with the residential-life office.

68: Is There Life After Classes?	Clubs and Organizations	Contact the director of student services or student life for this information.
69: May I Take Classes Abroad?	Study-Abroad Opportunities	Contact the Study-Abroad office to learn about available options.
70: Is it Possible to Play a Sport in College?	Athletics	Contact the athletics department, or check the website.
71: May I Practice My Faith in College?	Religious Observance	Contact the campus ministry or interfaith department to get a list of all available religious options.
72: What Happens After May 1st?	Post Deposit	Contact the admission office for this information.

Question	Topic	How to Get Answers
73: What Happens During Orientation?	Student Orientation	Check with the office that handles orientation.
74: Is There a Program for My Parents?	Parent Orientation	Check with the office that handles orientation.
75: What Courses Will I Take in the First Semester?	Registration	Contact the registrar's office.
76: What Is My "Academic Bible"?	Catalog	Get a hard copy of the catalog from the registrar's office.

77: May I Use My Smartphone or Tablet in Class?	Classroom Rules	Review the information in the school catalog.
78: What Happens If I Have to Leave School?	Leave of Absence	The catalog will outline the procedures to follow if you have to withdraw from school or take a leave of absence.
79: When Does School Stop and Start?	Four-Year Calendar	Check the website or catalog, or contact the registrar's office.
80: Do I Need a Doctor's Note to Begin School?	Health Regulations	Contact the health office for a list of required immunizations.

Question	Topic	How to Get Answers
81: What Happens If Parents Lose Their Jobs?	Changes in Family Finances	Contact your financial aid counselor if your family's finances have changed.
82: May I Pay My Tuition in Installments?	Payment Plans and Financing Options	Contact the bursar's office for a list of all available options.
83: Should I Get a Job in College?	Employment	Either the financial aid office or the cooperative-education office can help with this question.
84: Do I Have to Complete All My High School Courses?	"Senioritis"	You already know the answer!

85: Should I Get a Car?	First Semester and "Wheels"	Check the catalog to find out whether freshman are even allowed to have cars. If so, consider the pros and cons with your parents.
86: Is It Normal to Feel Homesick?	Homesick	Many students feel homesick at first, but if homesickness stops you from making friends or going to classes, contact the office responsible for counseling services that is listed on the website.
87: Is It Normal for Parents to Miss Their Child?	Empty Nest	Parents usually adjust over time but should seek counseling if that is not the case.

Question	Topic	How to Get Answers
88: Should I Work Even If I Don't Get Paid?	Internships	Check on the website for the office that handles internships, or contact the career services department.
89: How Can I Prepare for Job Interviews?	Company Interviews	Contact the career services department for a list of the most recent company interviewers.
90: How Much Debt Is Too Much?	Debt Ratios and Starting Salaries	Contact the financial aid office for help with this question.
91: Is It OK to Go to Graduate School Right After College?	Graduate Schools	Contact the academic dean's office for information.

92: Is It OK to Go to Professional School Right After College?	Professional Schools	Contact the academic dean's office for information.
93: How Can I Stay Connected to My School After Graduation?	Free Courses	Contact the alumni office for this information.
94: Who Do I Communicate with After Graduation?	Alumni Office	The alumni office is your best contact.

PART 3: POST-GRADUATION STAGE		
Question	**Topic**	**How to Get Answers**
95: Employed, Unemployed, or Underemployed?	Jobs at Graduation	Contact the career office for the latest statistics.
96: Employed, Unemployed, or Underemployed After Six Months?	Jobs After Six Months	Contact the career office for the latest statistics.
97: May I Contact Alumni to Help Me Find a Job?	Alumni Connections	Contact the alumni office for this information.

98: Will I Hear from Someone in My Graduating Class?	Class Agents	Contact the alumni office for the names and contact numbers for the alumni agents for your class.
99: How Will My School Stay Connected to Me After Graduation?	School Connections	Contact the alumni office for more information.
100: Is There Anything More I Need to Find Out?	Getting Answers	Refer to this chart when you need help finding a job or considering further schooling.

BIBLIOGRAPHY

Bok, Derek. *Higher Education in America.* New Jersey: Princeton University Press, 2013.

Bowen, William. *Higher Education in the Digital Age.* New Jersey: Princeton University Press, 2013.

_____. Matthew M. Chingos, and Michael McPherson. *Crossing the Finish Line.* New Jersey: Princeton University Press, 2009.

Cantron, Marvin and Owen Davies. "50 Trends Shaping the Future." *World Future Society,* 2003.

Carlson, Scott, and Goldie Blumenstyk. "College Reinvented." *The Chronicle of Higher Education.* December 21, 2012.

_____. "Is College Worth It? 2 New Reports Says Yes (Mostly)." *The Chronicle of Higher Education.* November 15, 2013.

Carnevale, Anthony P., Nicole Smith and Jeff Strohl. *Help Wanted and Projections of Jobs and Education Requirements Through 2018.* Washington, D.C.: Georgetown Center on Education and the Workforce, 2010.

Christensen, Clayton M., and Henry J. Eyring. *The Innovative University.* San Francisco: Jossey-Bass, 2011.

College Board. *Knocking at the College Door.* December, 2003.

_____. *Trends in College Pricing 2013.* October, 2013.

Cowen, Tyler. *Average Is Over.* New York: Penguin, 2013.

Delbanco, Andrew. *College What It Was, Is, and Should Be.* New Jersey: Princeton University Press, 2012.

Dennis, Marguerite J., "Looking Ahead: Mega-Trends in Student Enrollment." *Recruitment and Retention in Higher Education* 18:1 (2004): 1+

_____. *Ten Trends in Higher Education.* Magna Publications, 2005.

Doubleday, Justin. "Earnings Gap Narrows but a Diploma Still Pays, Report Says." *The Chronicle of Higher Education,* October 18, 2013.

Friedman, Thomas L., and Michael Mandelbaum. *That Used to Be Us.* New York: Farrar, Straus and Giroux, 2011.

Ginder, Scott A. and Janice E. Kelly-Reid. *Postsecondary Institutions and Cost of Attendance in 2012-13; Degrees AND Other Awards Conferred, 2011-12; and 12-Month Enrollment, 2011-12.* U.S. Department of Education, May, 2013.

Halligan, Tom. "The Dismal State of Graduation Rates." *University Business,* April, 2004.

Jaschik, Scott. "Debt, Jobs, Diversity and Who Gets In: A Survey of Admissions Directors." *Inside Higher Education,* November 6, 2013.

_____. "Jobs, Value and Affirmative Action: A Survey of Parents About College." *Inside Higher Education,* March 20, 2013.

Kiley, Kevin. "Short-term Focus, Long-Term Problems: A Survey of Business Officers." *Inside Higher Education,* July 27, 2012.

Laurent, Clint. *Tomorrow's World.* Singapore: John Wiley & Sons, 2013.

Lawlor Report. "Survey Findings-- Affordability Is Top Marketplace Challenge, According to College Administrators." 2013.

Levine, Arthur, and Diane R. Dean. *Generation on a Tightrope.* San Francisco: John Wiley & Sons, 2012.

Martin, Andrew. "Downturn Still Squeezes Colleges and Universities." *The New York Times,* January 14, 2013.

McCluskey, Frank Bryce, and Melanie Lynn Winter. *The Idea of the Digital University: Ancient Traditions, Disruptive Technologies and the Battle for the Soul of Higher Education.* Washington, D.C.: Westphalia Press, 2012. January, 2010.

Moody's Investor Service, "Annual Sector Outlook for U.S. Higher Education for 2010." January, 2010.

National Center for Education Statistics. *Postsecondary Institutions and Cost of Attendance in 2012-13.* Washington, D.C., 2013.

National Student Clearinghouse Research Center. Term Enrollment Estimates. Fall, 2012-2013.

Newman, Frank, Lara Couturier and Jamie Scurry. *The Future of Higher Education: Rhetoric, Reality and the Risks of the Market.* San Francisco: Jossey-Bass, 2004.

Raby, Rosalind Latiner, and Edward J. Valeau, Editors. *Community College Models.* California: Springer, 2009.

Schwarz, Emily. "One-third of US colleges facing falling or stagnant tuition revenue." Moody's Investors Service, Inc., January 14, 2013.

Selingo, Jeffrey J. *College (Un) Bound.* New York: Houghton Mifflin, 2013.

Sloan Consortium. "Changing Course: Ten Years of Tracking Online Education in the United States." January 16, 2013.

Thompson, Andy. "Student Loan Default Rates Continue a Steady Climb." *The Chronicle of Higher Education.* October 11, 2013.

Vander Ark, Tom. *Getting Smart How Digital Learning Is Changing The World.* San Francisco: Jossey-Bass, 2012.

Zemsky, Robert. *Checklist for Change Making American Higher Education a Sustainable Enterprise.* New Jersey: Rutgers University Press, 2013.